A Life, With Dogs

A Life, With Dogs

A Chapbook, Memoir in Fragments

Brad Owens

Meadows and Hart Publishing

CONTENTS

CONTENTS

A Place Back Home

There is a place back home,
near my parents' house,
in the mountains.
It's a tiny nook tucked
behind bramble
and blackberry thorns;

Sequestered.

I would go there
in winter.
Crossing dead weeds
and brush,
I would make my way
towards the wild.
Over the frozen creek bed,
through the maze of stilled life,

into icy space.

I would sit and dream.

Watching frigid water
gurgle downwards,
searching for the sea.
Or so I imagined amidst
Sleeping trees,
Surreal,
Silent,
I wished
I could
flow
like
water
to
new
lands,
be
free,
be
me.
Thinking on it now,
that place back home,
I wonder what a trip there might cost.

2 |

...With Dogs, Nicky and Monty

My father died. It was October 4th, a Thursday afternoon, at 1:30. It was years ago now, but I'm still angry. I blame the Veteran's hospital for trying ineffective chemo; they said there was a chance and I think they lied. I blame the military for using Agent Orange during Vietnam; my father used to talk about the clouds that fell from the sky all around him. I blame America for allowing us to go to Vietnam in the first place; shouldn't we have known better? I was angry at the world; how was cancer still a thing? I was angry at myself.

My father was in the hospital bed that hospice care sent to his house when he died, and he was crowded by armchairs and end tables, kitchen chairs and folding chairs and anything else that could serve as seating. Every seat was taken. My father had, has, a lot of family. They all came at one time or another, and many stayed.

The room where they put the bed was an addition,

complete with big French doors that could easily, when both were opened, accommodate a stretcher and was a direct shot to the driveway. An ambulance could back up to the door, no fuss, no bother. The whole room, in fact, the whole situation, the whole year before reeked of my parents' innate ability to make things easier for those around them. My father, in particular, thought about others, cared about others, more than he cared about himself, mostly.

I had tried to learn that lesson, the lesson of caring about the comfort of others, but it was always so very difficult. I often wondered if Dad felt the struggle too. It didn't show, at least with his family. Everyone was welcome at Dad's house, leave your shoes on, sit anywhere you like, and it was the same with strangers as it was with family.

On the day my father died, the nurse arrived for his daily care routine, which included shaving, around 1:00. Usually, someone else, my mother, one of my aunts, helped the nurse shave him, but for some reason, possibly no reason, possibly every reason, they were all doing other things. Mom hadn't eaten that day, so someone brought a pizza. My aunts and cousins were all eating. I wasn't eating. I was helping the nurse shave my father's beard.

I remember moving along the side of the bed closest to the wall, I remember the tight space between the wall and the bed frame, I remember banging my shin on the heavy metal machinery that made up the undercarriage of the bed, and I remember the smell of antiseptics and bleach. That was my gift, my personal and individual strength-I remembered everything.

The nurse had the shaving supplies laid out on a table next to the bed. The smell of the shaving cream, like soap made of air, mingled with the bleach and disinfectant as she smeared it along his chin, his cheeks, the loose skin of his neck. I could barely look at him like this. He had lost so much weight, so much weight. I held Dad's skeletal head while she maneuvered the razor around his cheek and chin. She only got half way through the shave when he stopped breathing. I noticed it first. The stillness, that unnatural softening of his face, told me something was wrong, and I looked toward Mom. I was still holding my father's head while the nurse rummaged through her things, looking for a stethoscope. My mother was sitting near the door, eating pizza. Between us, my aunts and uncles and cousins and strangers talked about mundane things. My voice didn't work.

"He's not breathing," the nurse said, pulling at the front of Dad's sheets and clothing, shoving the metal bell of the device through the neck of his t-shirt. It was odd to see Dad in a loose fitting shirt. He hated that. For as long as I could remember, he wore shirts that fit. Never oversized, never stretched out, and never over-washed; they always fit. Now, when he was too weak to protest, he had a giant shirt on, one that accommodated his neck and the nurse's hand, and it still left room for her to maneuver all around his chest. He would have hated that shirt. I only realized later that it was one of his shirts. He had lost so much weight, so much weight. So much.

I held his head. It was the last thing I did while he was still alive. It felt like I needed to keep doing it. His eyes fluttered open, then he gasped. He was breathing again, but in short, gulping staccato, the pain etched on his face, his eyes wide and wild.

"He's struggling to breathe," the nurse said, and I wondered who she was talking to. She kept moving the stethoscope around, settling on different places for a moment and then moving to another one. I held dad's head. He stopped breathing again, and this time, the shift, that unnatural calm, was deeper, more shocking, and tinged with barbed wire that circled my own chest. I couldn't breathe.

"He's gone," the nurse said.

Mom's scream filled the house. The slice of pizza she had been holding fell to the floor as my aunts surrounded her, hugging, keeping her upright, and helping her to the side of the bed.

"Tell him it's okay to go," the nurse told me.

I tried. It came out sounding like someone else's voice, someone else's intent, someone else's belief, "It's okay."

What a ridiculous last thing to say to my father. It wasn't like me at all.

It took a long time for things to progress after that, but I do remember that the nurse made sure to take all of dad's medication with her before she left.

"They sure do get them drugs back," my cousin said and I wondered if she wanted them herself. There were rumors, but I didn't care about that now. I really didn't care about anything much. I wandered the house. Everywhere I went there were people, family, crowding every nook. My two little Pekingese dogs were there. My aunt held one. The other was following me. I scooped the one out of my aunt's lap and went to my bedroom. The other followed. I closed the door and lowered myself to the plush carpet. I curled up there. My dogs nestled in with me and I cried until sleep came.

3

A Fascination with the Circus

"It's a big tent where they have big rings on the ground," his mother had explained the day before, tracing circles in the air as she did so.

"How big is the tent?" he had asked.

"Bigger than our whole house. Big enough for a whole bunch of elephants to fit in."

His 6-year old mind had filled to bursting. The rest of the day had been spent trying to conjure a realistic image of a giant tent big enough to hold a herd of elephants. He couldn't quite accomplish it; instead, he went to bed and allowed sleep to paint the picture. He had repeated the name of the circus as he drifted off to sleep... the Ringling Brothers and Barnum and Bailey Circus, the Ringling Brothers and Barnum and Bailey Circus, the Ringling...

Time ticked on while Brad stayed in bed. "The Ringling Brothers and Barnum and Bailey Circus," he whispered one last time. Finally, he couldn't wait any longer. He got up and dressed, picking his favorite Bugs Bunny t-shirt and jeans. In the kitchen, he pulled a chair over to the counter and climbed up to reach the cabinet with the cereal. It was a special day so he picked the BooBerry instead of Raisin Bran. After he ate, he put his bowl into the sink and went to the bathroom where he brushed his teeth. Then, he sat on the sofa, turned on early morning cartoons, and waited.

"You're up early," Dave suddenly said from the kitchen. "Got something important to do today?"

He wasn't sure how to answer. Had his father forgotten about the circus? His heart felt heavy in his chest.

"If you don't got nothing better to do, maybe we should go to the circus," Dave said, winking, as he rubbed his son's head and slurped his coffee. "You brush your teeth?"

Brad nodded, smiling a smile so wide that it hurt his cheeks.

"Alright, let me drink my coffee and we'll go."

The drive to the circus took far too long. Brad was so excited that he forgot to hold his father's hand as they walked toward the enormous striped tent. His mother had been right-it was big enough for a herd of elephants. She hadn't mentioned the rest though. The game booths, where you could win stuffed animals, played tinkling music that felt like sparkles of light inside his head. Each one slightly different, at different tempos, making a cacophony of sparkly sound. The sweet scent of candy permeated the air, mixed with the warm smells of roasted peanuts and hot dogs. As they neared the tent, another smell greeted him. This one earthy, pungent, like the cow pastures when they went for a drive in the country, but different somehow. More substantial.

Inside the tent, the excitement continued. New music, deeper, more important, reverberated all around, flashing lights, every color he knew, made him smile that painful, wonderful smile. The sounds of other children laughing and squealing with delight, barkers yelling their wares up and down the bleacher rows, his father talking loudly with the other fathers. It was all so much, nearly too much for a child so used to a small, quiet apartment in the suburbs of Chicago. With Mom working days and Dad working nights, there was always a need for the son to be quiet. Even when Dad was awake, his PTSD from Vietnam demanded a quiet child. Brad was so used to being quiet that he couldn't bring himself to make noise, even in this atmosphere.

Instead, he watched, wide-eyed and giddy.

The lights dimmed and the show began. New colors swirled from lights hidden in the heights of the tent's vaulted ceiling. The music crescendoed, the ringmaster began his announcements. Brad inched to the edge of his seat, pushing his toes to the wooden floor. Then, the clowns appeared.

One looked like Bozo from the early morning t.v. show. His bright red hair jutted out like a crescent moon stuck to his head. Brad wondered where Clara Bell was. There was another, with a giant puffball of red, like Ronald McDonald. Brad turned to his father to ask what these clowns' names were, but he was talking with a new friend and sneaking drinks from the concealed whiskey bottle between his feet. The clowns came closer. They weren't like the television clowns at all. They were men, mostly, dressed like clowns. He was confused. Why would a grown man dress like that? It made no sense. Men were serious, somber, scary. One came closer and Brad could smell the sweat and the makeup. He sank down in his seat and tried to become invisible, like he did at home.

The clowns retreated after a seemingly impromptu performance with water buckets full of confetti, and Brad felt it was safe to watch the center rings again; but he was aware they were still there, in the shadows, waiting. Two rows over, a barker was selling peanuts.

"Here," Dave said, thrusting money into his little hand. The smell of the whiskey on his breath was dizzying. "Go get me some peanuts."

Brad took the money and slid from the safety of his seat.

Keeping an eye out for an errant clown, he gripped the railing and walked down the steps. They were too wide for him to go one foot after the other so he had to step together, step together, down toward the rings.

"And now," the ring master's voice filled the tent loud. "Make no sudden moves. Keep your children close..."

Brad turned and looked back up the row where his father was taking another swig and laughing with his friend.

"Because," the ringmaster continued, "entering the center ring..."

Brad looked at the money in his hand. He needed to get peanuts. Step together, step together. The center ring, just on the other side of a fluttering net, came alive with rapidly moving circles of light. Step together. The front row, just feet from a large pedestal, was now eye level with Brad's small frame.

"The most dangerous animals on the planet," the ring master boomed and tigers came bounding from multiple directions. One of the large cats leapt and perched on the pedestal in front of Brad. Their eyes met and the great cat licked its lips.

"Keep calm and remember, no sudden moves," the ring master said. The cat lowered its head and sniffed, its mouth slightly open, fangs glinting in the spotlight. Brad froze. Fear ensnared him, swallowed him down. He began to back slowly. Step together. The cat watched him with interest. Step together. He stumbled back up the steps.

A loud crack caused Brad's heart to skip and the cat turned away and faced the center of the ring. Seeing his chance, Brad turned and ran as fast as he could up the stairs and back to his seat.

He sat, trying desperately to be invisible, but his father could always see him. Find him, even when he hid in the closet. Dave saw the unused wad of money in the tiny hand. He huffed and snatched the money back as he turned and laughed with his friend.

Brad swallowed to keep from crying. Boys don't cry He tried to watch the show, especially when the elephants replaced the tigers. There were so many lights and such happy looking people all around, but all he could feel was a desperate desire to leave. To go back to his room and sit quietly with books and personal thoughts. He watched his father take another drink and something else struck him, a feeling, a thought, so complex, so dark, that his young mind refused to ponder it for long. He made himself as small as he could in his seat, sat quietly amid the cheering crowd, and thought about what it would take to grow up and join the circus.

$$4$$

...With Dogs, Lacy

I eventually got into my bed and had a fitful sleep. I knew that sleep was not what was expected of me. I was supposed to be in with the family, cryingor laughing, or, hell, I didn't know what to do. I did not want to be around anyone. My dogs needed to go outside though, so I opened the bedroom door and my father was standing in the kitchen making breakfast.

My legs went weak until I noticed that the frame wasn't quite right, that the stance was just a bit off. It was my uncle, one of dad's brothers, and the pain redoubled. Most everyone had gone by that point, but several aunts and uncles remained. I took my dogs outside.

I watched them happily smell everything and pee on everything they could. They were fine, just like always and I wished that I could be fine again, but I feared I never would. I was suddenly a child again, lost, alone, afraid of everything, and my father was not there to keep the fears at bay, like he had in Illinois.

My first dog, at least the first I could remember, was Lacy.

She was a black and white toy collie that became my only companion as a child in the suburbs of Chicago. There was a period of time, just a couple of hours, between when my father left for the night shift and my mother came home from work, that I spent alone in our house. I would walk home with some older kids from the neighborhood, those in fourth or fifth grade, and use the key on a chain around my neck to let myself into the house. The other kids would continue on toward the end of the cul-de-sac.

We would play the games, me and Lacy, that I saw on the Bozo show. I would line up paper cups in a long row and then I would try to toss a ping-pong ball into the first cup. Lacy would chase the ball if I missed and hold it in her mouth. She never bit down, but I always had to pry it out of her mouth to get it back. If I made it into the cup, she would stare down into it and wait for me to get the ball out. I practiced every-day just in case Bozo ever invited me on his show to play the real game.

After Bozo, we watched Casper, the Friendly Ghost, and I always told the t.v. that I would be Casper's friend whenever the animated children ran from him. Then, Lacy and I would run around the sofa and chase each other. After that, Romper Room came on, I didn't care much for their games, Bozo's were better, but I waited for the end when Miss Elizabeth would say who she saw in the magic mirror. One time, I remember distinctly, she said, "I see Brad." I was shocked.

She could see me. It had to be me. Miss Elizabeth saw me through her magic mirror. I yelled and Lacy barked. It was very exciting.

Lacy and I would also go in the backyard. I wasn't allowed in the front yard because of the road, but the back yard was fenced in and Lacy needed to go to the bathroom. I would try to get dandelions up by the roots. That was one of my chores when Mom and I did yard work. I carefully pulled just one at a time because I had tried to pull up a whole bunch once. I grabbed the base of a big clump and pulled and pulled. The dandelions stayed in the ground and the bee that was hidden in the stalks got really mad. I cried, but Lacy licked my hand until it felt better.

My parents took Lacy away one day. I was very confused about the whole thing, but I remember them saying they couldn't take her where we were going. I cried night and day until Dad suddenly showed up with Lacy in the car. She and I ran around the front yard until we, or rather I, collapsed from joy. Lacy kept running around. We moved to Virginia soon after that.

Lacy was spooked by fireworks during our first summer in Virginia. She ran off into the woods and I never saw her again. I blamed my father. After all, he was the one who wanted to move back closer to his family. He was the one who wanted to live in the woods, in the middle of nowhere, with nothing but trees all around us. He was the one who didn't have a plan for this big move so Lacy had to stay outside because my grandmother didn't believe in having animals in the house. So, my only friend died alone in the unfamiliar woods of Virginia, and I blamed my father. After all, I was six years old and I needed to blame someone.

5

Moving to Virginia

The red Cadillac his father drove sat in the driveway next to the moving truck his uncle was going to drive, as Brad sat in the backseat and waited. The white, leather seats were cool to the touch. He gazed at the silver fixture holding the door's handle and smiled. It was his friend, the amorphous blob that lived in the car.

The blob flitted and pulsed under the early morning sun. Brad giggled, softly, very quietly, as his little friend moved from the silver door handle to the lock, where he did a little dance. It reminded Brad of Casper, The Friendly Ghost, which he had watched every afternoon after school. The blob continued to dance as Dave and Lorine climbed into the front seats.

"You sure you got everything?" Lorine asked as Dave brought the car to life.

"Yep," he replied and they were off. Soon, the suburbs of Chicago were in the rear window, retreating rapidly.

Brad thought of his friends, his teacher, his neighborhood. They weren't sad thoughts, not really. They were inevitable thoughts. His parents told him they were moving. That was the end of that. Brad had not questioned the decision, and he didn't question it now as the Cadillac turned onto the interstate to head out of Illinois.

They had taken this trip many times before. Brad remembered Christmas trips and summer vacations in Virginia. They had always been fun. He liked spending time with his cousins, his grandparents, his aunts and uncles. There always seemed to be family around in Virginia, not like Illinois.

The blob continued to dance along the silver trim on the door panel. Brad smiled and held out his finger. The blob swirled around his tiny digit, and Brad imagined he had tickled his car friend.

On day two of the trip, the buildings and long stretches of road gave way to mountains and curves. Brad looked up into the sky and could only see a tiny spot of blue in between the green. It was so different from the outskirts of the city where the sky seemed so big until it met the shores of the lake and turned into the green-blue of the water; the flatness creating the illusion of connectedness. Here, nothing was flat. Here, the sky seemed so small and so far away.

His friend fluttered in the door handle. He had become smaller too. The edges of his white form became tinted with the green that seemed to dominate everything here in these strange mountains.

"What time do we need to get there?" Lorine asked, breaking the silence that had permeated the car for hours on end.

"About another hour." Dave replied.

Brad listened to his parents, like he always did. Being quiet was the rule of the house, ever since his father had punched a hole in the wall after Brad had poked him to ask for cereal. "You need to be careful," his mother had told him. "No loud noises. Don't sneak up on him." Brad took the admonitions to heart. He was a quiet child, perhaps the quietest that had ever been.

The car slowed and turned into a parking lot that went straight up from the winding two lane road. Brad watched his friend suddenly get much whiter. He looked healthier without all the green outlining him. Brad smiled.

"Here we are. Everyone out," Dave said with a barely contained giddiness that he Brad had never heard before.

Lorine helped Brad out of the backseat and the family walked toward a building that reminded Brad of the car wash his father would take him to on some Sundays. It had lots of windows and cars were parked everywhere. Finally, something seemed familiar.

"Y'all wait here," Dave instructed. "I'll get the keys."

Lorine sat on a bench beside the front door. Brad stood next to her. Up close, this building was nothing like the ones in the city. It was covered in black dust, and the green grew out of the roof, like a fungus, before it joined the mountain just behind. Brad looked across the two lane road and another mountain shot up into the sky just on the other side.

"Here we go," Dave suddenly said, emerging from the glass door. He was pointing to a large, black truck. Brad climbed awkwardly into the middle of the long seat and put his feet to the side of the gear shift. His mother climbed in next to him and his father appeared behind the steering wheel. There were no silver surfaces at all.

6

...With Dogs, Sam

Years later, after several dogs that were never quite the same as Lacy, I made a discovery in my father's Vietnam War memorabilia. He often let me play with his medals. They didn't seem to mean that much to him. It would be many more years before I realized he was trying to forget. As a child, I couldn't forget anything. It seemed to be my curse. I remembered things that my parents completely forgot. I remembered my father making me clean up my own vomit when I was sick because he couldn't stand the smell and Mom was working. I remember being locked out of the apartment in Chicago, the one we lived in before the suburban house, when I was in Kindergarten and having to wait on the steps until Mom got off work only to find out that my father was asleep in the apartment the whole time. I remembered going to the bars on the weekends, watching my father drink from early morning until late in the evening. I would sit and listen to the jukebox and listen to the drunks talk. I remembered everything.

As I was looking through his keepsakes from the war, the medals, the letters of commendation, the letters from home, old photographs, I found a Polaroid of my father as a young man. He was dressed in the fatigues I recognized from old movies, his hair was shorn on the sides and a little longer on top, which was odd because he had been bald for as long as I could remember, and he was sitting with a black and white dog between his legs. The dog reminded me so much of Lacy that I immediately became angry. He seemed to love this dog, maybe as much as I loved Lacy, and that seemed unfair to me. I didn't even have a single picture of me and Lacy, but I remembered. I remembered everything.

The old picture of my father with his dog in Vietnam haunted me. I had never thought of animals in the war. The history I had been taught certainly didn't mention dogs. I was confused by the photo. It seemed so anachronistic, so wrong. Soon after I found the photo, Sam, the Siberian Husky who always played ball with me in the yard, slinked off into the woods and died.

"I bet he was poisoned," my father whispered to my uncle when we all found Sam.

Poisoned? Who would poison a dog? It seemed the most evil thing I had ever heard. I watched my uncle and my father lift the stiff-legged remains of my dog and put him into a large garbage bag, which would serve as his coffin.

"It was probably someone up on Rakes Ridge," Uncle Ural said.

Rakes Ridge always seemed so far away. There were strange people who lived up there that we blamed for everything.

They lived on top of the mountain and we lived on the side. Whenever a fence broke, their cows would wander down into our yards. Many of the houses, without city water, still emptied their septic tanks onto our side of the mountain. Most of the waste sunk into the ground well before it reached us, but it was the idea that was disturbing. Dad and Ural carried the garbage bag between them as we made our way back to Grandma's yard. I remembered the day I found out how Sam liked to play tether ball. Alone on the side of the mountain in Virginia, I would often try and entertain myself with made-up games. My grandparents had a tether ball set at the end of the yard. I would swing the ball around its pole, watching the orange-yellow rope twine around the metal. Then, once the ball hit and bounced off the pole, I would push it the other way trying to make it go faster with each rotation. A simple game, but a way to pass the lonely hours.

One day, Sam saw me playing tether ball alone. He came up next to me and as I began to twist the rope, he jumped up and hit the ball with his nose sending it back in my direction. I was astonished.

"Dad! Dad!" I yelled across the yard to the porch where my father sat in the shade with my grandmother. "Watch this!" And I sent the ball back around for Sam to hit. I turned and saw my grandmother fanning herself with an old paper church fan and my father dismissively wave as they continued to talk. It didn't matter that they were unimpressed. Sam and I would spend hours from that day on playing tether ball in the yard.

I stood nearby as my father dug the hole that would be

Sam's resting place and I watched as my uncle unceremoniously dumped the bag into the hole. They both worked to fill in the dirt and the impromptu funeral was over. I walked behind my father and uncle until we came to the edge of my grandmother's yard. A few years later, Dad took down the tether ball pole, no one played anymore, and planted a pine tree I got from the 4H Club.

7

A Belief in Santa Claus

I never really believed
in Santa Claus.
Not really
even though I tried.
I lacked the faith
to accept the unacceptable,
to believe the unbelievable,
to listen to the lies.
Reindeer could not fly,
otherwise, I could.
I wanted it badly enough,
I prayed for it strongly enough,
to float into the sky
on wings
of belief
and trust
and truth.

At some point,
as I grew older,
I gave up wanting to fly,
I gave up looking for presents
from fictional men,
and I no longer waited for
answers from the sky.

8

...WIth Dogs, Snoopy

Snoopy was a beagle, named for the cartoon, of course. He was large for a beagle, or at least he seemed large to me. He followed me wherever I went. From our trailer set into the side of the mountain, to my grandparents' house, to the rhododendron patches, to the top of the mountain where the cliffs produced long, deep shadows on the valley where my father's entire family lived.

I had almost completely forgotten my time in the suburbs of Chicago by the time Snoopy came around. My accent had shifted enough that no one asked where I was from anymore. I was a native Virginian for all intents and purposes. I liked to walk in the woods surrounding our trailer. It was a different world. The sun stabbing through the leafy canopy always seemed like tiny spotlights leading me to new discoveries. I would follow the sunlight deep into the forest, followed closely by Snoopy who would periodically howl and run off down a side path only to return panting happily. I never knew what he was chasing. For all I knew, he might have been just playing a game.

The rhododendron fields were about half a mile past the yard of my parents' house. I went there often as a child. The heavy trunks of the ancient plants lifted the foliage above the ground so that the entire field was a makeshift fort. I would climb beneath the deep green leaves and find a place where I could sit up straight. There I would dream of leaving the mountains, getting out of nowhere, going somewhere, any-where that wasn't the mountains. It really didn't matter where I would go, the ocean was always on the list, but wherever I would go had to be better than the intense loneliness of the mountains.

I had cousins, lots of cousins, but they all lived away from my grandparents. We lived on the same mountain, just a few hundred feet from them. So, my cousins would only come on the weekends. My friends from school never visited. The drive up the mountain road was too difficult for anything other than a four-wheel drive, so they stayed away. After a while I stopped inviting them. So, most of the time, it was just me, Snoopy, and the mountain.

I found an old cigar tin in my grandfather's shed. I cut out pictures from magazines and kept them safe in the tin underneath the rhododendron. I would take the pictures out and decorate my fort under the rhododendron. I had maga-zine pages of paintings of the grandmasters, antique clocks, advertisements that I thought were artistic, and people. I would place them around the rhododendron room, each one greeted by a sniff from Snoopy, until I felt the room was well furnished.

Then, I would dream.

Snoopy wandered off one day. When night came, he was still not back. That was unusual. He never stayed away all night. Dad went to look for him the next day. He returned carrying a garbage bag.

That night, I watched as my father dug a hole.

"Dogs like to go off alone when they die," Dad said as he dug. I nodded as he handed me the shovel to finish digging the grave. Dad unceremoniously dropped the bag into the hole and we covered it with dirt. Back home, I went to my room as mom and dad settled in to watch the six o'clock news on television.

Shopping Therapy

I'd like to flip off the entire world.
Instead, I buy a hat on credit.

I push all my anger and resentment
through a magnetic tape reader,

or I offer up an app from my phone
or my watch and I delight

in the technology and the materialism.
A sensible thought invades,

"You won't wear this."
"Fuck it!" I scream,

adding a braided belt,
a pair of discounted shoes to the total .

Car Country

It was burnt orange,
the Chevy Citation,
my first car.
There was an electrical problem
that caused it to burst into flames
on my way home from high school one day.
We watched the car burn
in the middle of the dirt road,
my parents and me.
Nothing to be done
but let the flames die out
eventually.
Afterwards, dad used the bull dozer
from the mine to push
the charred remains
over the edge of the road.
It rolled five,

ten,
twenty
feet down
where it joined other cars
that had met similar fates.
My grandfather's truck was there,
the one with the bad transmission.
My uncle's lemon,
the one he still complains about,
sat half buried in kudzu.
Dad had two cars over this cliff.
One he wrecked;
One, I don't know.
And now, my burnt orange
burnt car is there too.
Years later
I'm struck by the idea
of disposed of cars in the mountains.
I wouldn't even think to throw one over the cliff now.
And years into the future,
when the mountains might not be as remote as they are,
will someone find those cars?
Will they wonder who owned them?
Will they judge us for dumping them over the cliff?
Will they know that the burnt one was mine?

11

...With Dogs, Luke

In graduate school, a couple of my friends and I went to the dog pound. We were going because my friend Lisa wanted to look for a dog. Leslie and I were there for moral support. I drove because I had my mother's hand-me-down SUV in case she got a big dog.

I had never been to a pound before. I wasn't prepared for the sadness I felt looking into the eyes of all of those dogs. I let Lisa and Leslie go off in their own direction while I watched a particularly sad looking dog that seemed like a shaggy version of Dorothy's Toto.

"You want to meet him?" the attendant asked.

"Uh, sure," I said as she opened the cage and let me in. The poor animal didn't move. I bent down and rubbed his head. He opened his eyes weakly but just readjusted and went back to sleep. "What's wrong with him?"

"He's just old. Probably won't last another week."

My heart cracked. I sat down on the floor and petted the

sleeping dog as I waited for Lisa to make her selection. I felt something behind me. I turned and saw a white dog with one ear standing straight up and the other bent permanently. He lowered his head and looked up at me.

"Well, hey you," I whispered. "I didn't even see you there." I put my arm around him and scratched his chest as I continued to pet the elderly dog. His nose moistened my hand as I scratched.

"Well, I'll be..." another attendant suddenly said as she was walking by. "That dog has never let anyone pet him before."

"What're you talking about, he can barely lift his head." "Not that one. The white one. He's terrified of people. We think he was abused. He won't even let me touch him."

Lisa couldn't decide on a dog, but I took a little white dog with funny ears home. The problem was that I was a graduate student living in an apartment that didn't take pets. I hadn't figured on that. Luke, I named him after Luke Skywalker, and I stayed quietly in my apartment until the weekend when I took him to my parents' house.

"We don't want another dog," my mother said.

"I'm sorry, I just couldn't leave him there. He wouldn't let anyone touch him but me. I had to."

"Well, he can have Mister's old house, I guess," Dad offered. Mister was another beagle Dad had while I was in college. He died a few weeks before, and I left Luke with my parents in Mister's house. I called a couple of days later and Luke and Dad had become fast friends. Mom told me that Dad let him in the house. He was the first dog my parents ever had in the house.

Luke and Dad became inseparable. Dad started by building Luke his own house, which was really the garden shed, and he spent every daylight minute with him in the shed. Mom was often there with them too. Everyone in town knew about Luke. Dad bragged on him to anyone who would listen.

"He's the best dog I ever had," Dad would say, "Except for Crash."

Talking about Luke was the first time I had ever heard the name, Crash. He never elaborated on Crash, but he began to mention him more and more. However, Luke was obviously the topic of most conversations now. By the time I finished grad school and got my first teaching position, everyone knew Luke better than me.

"How're you doing?" the woman at the grocery store would ask whenever I would stop in for a soda before heading up the mountain to my parents' house. It was the same grocery store where I took Grandma once a month from the moment I could drive until I left for college. We would buy so many groceries that we filled two shopping carts to overflowing and stuffed the back of the truck with bags.

"I'm good. How are you?" I would respond.

"I'm good," the woman would continue. "How's Connie doing?"

Connie was my aunt, and I realized that the woman who had seen me for years thought I was my cousin Brian. "She's fine." I would rather say than correct her. After all, I usually knew if Connie wasn't fine.

More often than not, when I got to my parents' house, Luke would greet me in the driveway and bark at my tires all the way to the house where Dad would be sitting in the garage with the door open.

"He won't let nothing in his yard. No other dogs, no deer, no turkeys, he don't even like bees flying over the grass," Dad would say, after I settled in and joined him in the garage. He was always amazed at how protective Luke had become of his home.

"The other day, your mom was washing dishes and I was sitting here, Luke started making the awfullest racket. I thought there must be a snake in the yard or something. He hates snakes. Kills 'em with one bite. Never seen the like."

I heard about Luke's exploits every time I called home. I heard how he was tougher than any other dog on the mountain, how he went everywhere with Dad, riding in Dad's golf cart, which he bought only to go to Grandma's house now that they moved to the top of the mountain. Luke was the talk of the family. The best dog anyone had ever seen.

"I yelled at your mom to get a hoe. I figured I'd help him kill the snake this time, he was still making a fuss. I took the hoe out and Luke was digging a ditch in the yard. The snake must have went down a hole, I thought. I got there and you won't believe it..."

I waited for Dad to tell me, but he was the master story teller. He waited for me to ask, "What was it?"

"An ant hill!" Dad exclaimed and his laugh filled the garage, loud and full. "He was trying to kill each ant as it came out of the hill."

I laughed with Dad. It was impossible not to laugh with Dad when he found something truly funny.

"Best dog I ever had, except for Crash."

"Crash?" I finally asked. He had been mentioning him for a while now. I figured it was time to know.

"Yep, Crash, the dog I had in Vietnam."

Crash. Crash was a Vietnamese dog. He was the dog from the picture I had found so many years before. The picture that made me hate my father for killing Lacy. I knew now that it wasn't his fault. As an adult, I received a fuller picture of the reasons we left Chicago. The crime, the violence, the sheer size of the place was too much for my small town parents. I understood much better now, being from the same small town. I had come to love the mountains, much like my father did, and I often felt unsettled outside of them.

"He came into camp one night and crawled into my bunk with me," Dad said through the telephone line. "Never seen the like. Vietnam people ate dogs back then, y'know? Never seen a dog just come right up to a person like that before."

He stopped telling me about Crash then, preferring to talk about Luke and what a great dog he had turned out to be.

I didn't get to go home as much as I wanted during the school year. I could go more often in the summers, and that was when Dad would tell me stories. He started telling me stories just about the time I left for college. I guess not having me around everyday made him a little nostalgic. At least, that's what I thought.

We would sit in the garage, which became Dad and Luke's hangout when the garden shed collected too many tools to be comfortable. In the summer, the garage door would stay open and we would sit just inside, out of direct sun, and talk.

Luke would travel between my chair and Dad's, wanting to be petted as much as possible. When one of us stopped, he would go to the other. When Mom joined us, she became part of the rotation.

When we weren't sitting in the garage, which Dad called the Dog House, and everyone else called Dad's Sitting Room, we would ride down the mountain on Dad's golf cart. Picking black berries all the way, to visit Grandma. Luke would run ahead and make sure the path was clear. We could hear him barking all through the mountains. He protected us from any possible danger his dog mind could identify. Dad took to bringing a hoe with us to help Luke kill the snakes along the way.

"I think he's Crash come back, the way he protects me," Dad offered one day.

"Yeah?" I asked, wondering what my very non-religious, but if you pressed him, Baptist, father thought about re-incarnation.

"Yep. I think Crash came back as Luke. He's just like him only white where Crash was black."

I nodded, although I still didn't know very much about Crash. From a lifetime of dealing with my father's particular brand of PTSD, I knew it was better to let him tell the story in his own time rather than ask questions. I stayed quiet and waited.

"He'd go on patrol with me. Every night after he showed up, he followed me everywhere. The other guys would feed him, but he stayed with me. Never left my side," Dad began.

A loud bark echoed through the mountains as Luke chased off a fox or a deer, making sure no animal came near us.

"Look there, some more black berries," Dad said, pointing to my side of the cart. I took the bucket that Mom had given us and started putting berries into it. It was nearly full and we were barely halfway to Grandma's so quite a few of them never made it into the bucket. I relished the sweetness of the berries and the warmth of the sun streaming through the trees. Dad took a handful from the bucket and ate them while I continued to pick.

"How many do we need for Grandma?" I asked.

"Just enough to make some jelly," Dad said between chews. "I'll get her some more later."

Luke suddenly darted out of the woods and stood in the middle of the cart path and panted happily.

"Go check the road," Dad said and motioned for Luke to leave. Luke jerked his head down and then up as if to acknowledge the order and then he took off down the path, barking loudly as he went.

"You sure have him trained," I said.

"Nope. He just started doing that himself one day. I tell you, he's Crash come back."

Just Before a Summer's Storm

Just before a summer storm,
The sky is dark and threatening,
The wind is turning leaves upside down,
You can smell the rain.
Prickly and exciting on your skin,
Sending alternating waves of comfort and fear
Cascading down your body,
You can feel the lightning.
Sensuous walls of warm air thrusts against you,
Moving over you, past and through you,
Like an amorous lover.
You can see the air.
Just before a summer storm,
The world is awash in anticipation,
Eager for the change to come,
Silent

Small Town Bookstore

For a shy, neurotic kid
growing up alone
on a mountain side
in Appalachia,
there is a magical place
in most every grocery store,

I would hurry through
the candy,
the toys,

"Now get what you want to eat,"
my mother would instruct.

Eating wasn't important.
The little wire rack filled with books was important.

Often, the rack would be near the magazines,
Sometimes it was near the register.
I would seek it out,
always.
I would find the one book
I was allowed per trip.
I had to be careful,
knowing the wrong choice
would mean nothing to read
until we needed milk.

And there is just so much milk a kid can drink.

In that little rack,
I found a rainbow
of colors when there was
only gray back home.

I found dreams
in books from
a little wire rack
in a grocery store
in the coalfields
in the mountains
of Virginia,
next to the paper towels.

14

...With Dogs, Luke
and Crash

It was Thanksgiving when Dad first noticed the knot on his collar bone.

"I guess I pulled something," he said. "I was helping out at the mine and this knot popped up." He pulled down the neck of his shirt and I could see the knot, about the size of a golf ball, just to the left of his neck.

"When you going to the doctor?" I asked, not giving him a chance to put it off.

"I got an appointment next week," he said and I felt better. It was nothing. I knew it was nothing. We sat in the garage, the door closed to the chill weather, and waited for Mom to finish getting ready to go to Grandma's for dinner. Luke snored softly in his bed between our chairs. Luke had gotten old. His teeth were falling out and one of his back legs no longer bent, but he still tried to follow wherever Dad went.

"Now, you stay," Dad said as he watched Luke struggle to get up when Mom came into the garage.

Luke gave up and settled back into his bed.

"We'll be right back," Mom told Luke as we left to get into the truck.

Dad drove and Mom sat in the middle. The radio played an old country tune that I knew by heart even though I never listened to country music anywhere other than my parents' house.

"He ain't gonna be around much longer," Dad said as we started off the mountain. Mom and I nodded, knowing he meant Luke. He was quiet for a long time. "I shouldn't have left Crash."

"Now Dave, you know you didn't have a choice," Mom offered and I got the sense this was a conversation I was joining in the middle.

"They ate dogs," Dad said and I could hear a catch in his throat. We started up the mountain road to Grandma's and the radio played another familiar song. I wondered if the radio station only had a certain number of songs they played over and over, and nothing from this century.

"How's your baby?" Mom asked, obviously referring to my dog Monty.

"He's fine," I said. "Spoiled rotten."

"That's what you're supposed to do," Dad said. We all nodded. The mountains looked gray with no leaves and no snow yet. The color seemed to have drained into the creek and flowed somewhere else. "He saved my life."

"Who did?" Mom asked.

"Crash," Dad continued, "One night on patrol. It was dark. Couldn't see nothing. I was crouched down next to a tree. It was raining. It always seemed to be raining. No moon, nothing."

The gray outside the window seemed to seep into the truck. I could feel the sorrow, the regret. The country song from the radio twanged in the background.

"Didn't even hear 'em. Got right up close behind me. Crash growled. Only way I knew he was there. Saved my life."

It was the most I'd ever heard my father talk of Vietnam. I knew from movies and history books and conversations with the other vets at the V.F.W. how bad it got, but the words of others never seemed to connect in my mind to my father. He never talked about the war. I wrongly supposed it was because he had nothing to say.

"I shouldn't have left him," Dad finished.

"The war was over. You had to leave," Mom said flatly and I got the sense that this conversation had long ago turned into an argument as Mom tried in vain to convince Dad that he had nothing to regret about the war. I had heard variations of the argument for a while now. Dad seemed to have reconciled what he was forced to do in the war, but this one thing, this dog, lingered.

Luke died less than a week before my father. Mom said it was past his time. He tried to hang on for Dad, but his body just wouldn't allow it. We buried him in the backyard just past the garden that he always guarded from crows and deer.

"I guess I won't be able to grow corn no more," Dad said after we finished. He was too weak to help. He simply laid in the hospital bed that hospice care brought for him. He could still talk, but weakly and in short intervals.

I brought Monty in to see him a couple of times. I placed the little white Pekingese on the side of his bed. Even when he was so weak he could barely open his eyes, Dad hugged Monty close. Monty was on his best behavior whenever Dad held him. He sat patiently as Dad weakly squeezed him.

The day Dad passed away, Monty wouldn't even come into the room. He sat outside and looked in, watching us all say goodbye. After the hospice people took back the bed, and the funeral home took Dad, we all sat in the living room. I tried not to cry, but it was too much. The years streamed before me.

Dad, young and angry, ignoring me for the most part, was gone. It was Dad, older, more in touch with his emotions, more caring than I had ever known him to be, that stayed. It was difficult to say goodbye to that Dad.

When everyone finally left, I realized I hadn't seen Monty for a while.

"Did he get outside?" Mom asked, and I panicked. The thought of my little Pekingese wandering around the woods made me ill. I rushed out into the night calling his name. Mom came with me. We walked everywhere the moonlight allowed. Nothing.

"Maybe he's in one of the back bedrooms," Mom offered.

We headed back inside, calling his name as we went from room to room. We found him, lying on the rug where Dad's hospital bed had been just hours before. He wouldn't leave. I had to go pick him up and carry him out of the room.

I found the picture of Dad with Crash again on the day of the funeral. We had already chosen the photo that would be displayed beside the coffin, or I would have suggested this one. He was so young, and posing with a dog seemed to be appropriate somehow. It was too late, and like so much of my relationship with Dad, I felt a pang of guilt. Did I choose the wrong photo? Could I have done better? Could I have done more? Always the same questions.

We had gone the week before to pick out a coffin. I didn't know how they showed the coffins to you. I wasn't prepared. One minute we were sitting in the office of the funeral home talking about the invoices and the next we walked down a hallway and into a room with dozens of coffins splayed out before us. I nearly lost it again. Why hadn't they told me I was going to a room full of coffins? Of course, they probably did and I didn't hear them. The whole week was a blur.

Mom walked slowly around the coffins, held up by my aunts as she went. I stopped at the door. I put my hand on the nearest coffin to steady myself and realized where my hand was. I jerked it back and tried to move further into the room. I couldn't. I stood at the door and watched Mom meander around. I needed to help, I knew this. But...and there it was, against the far wall, directly across from the door, an oak casket. Dad loved oak. It was his favorite wood. I had no idea why, and I had no idea why I knew that, but I did and it was.

The oak casket was the one we chose, but sitting in the sanctuary, looking at it, I wondered if I made the right decision. Should I have picked something else, something more expensive, but he loved oak, didn't he? Had I convinced myself of something that wasn't true? The questions never stopped.

Mom was in no condition to choose anything, and I tried my best. The music, eventually, was chosen by my uncles and aunts. I had no idea what he would want, other than George Jones, which I was sure wasn't appropriate for a traditional Baptist funeral. Donations to the Cancer Society instead of flowers, sure, that seemed like a good idea, but on the day, I regretted that decision. There should have been more flowers. He deserved more flowers. And the casket. And that picture.

I should have chosen the one with Crash, or maybe one with Luke, or, I think, there was one with Sam, or there was the one with Snoopy snuggled up to Dad's leg, or there was one with me and Monty and Dad. I should have chosen one with a dog in it. I should have, but I didn't.

We passed by the little table the funeral home had put at the entrance with a book people could sign. Above the table was the picture we had chosen of dad, sitting on grandma's porch. And behind the sign-in book was the picture of dad and Crash.

"I thought we could have more than one picture," Mom said as we walked down to the front row.

15

Saturdays at the Bar

"Can I have a quarter?" Brad asked from the bar stool next to his father, his little feet dangling above the metal tube that served as a footrest, not even close to touching it...yet.

Without looking up, acknowledging the question, or interrupting the conversation he was having with the woman behind the bar, Dave handed his son the change, the result of paying cash for beer, that sat on the bar in front of him. Brad took the coins and counted. Three quarters. There were others, but they wouldn't work in the jukebox, so he left them on the bar.

The coins clasped in his fist, Brad stretched his feet toward the floor and then let himself slide from the stool. The floor of the bar was sticky, probably due to the night before, from a Friday night in the Chicago suburbs. The jukebox sat by the front door, the red and yellow neon stripes forming a glowing rainbow. He knew which song he wanted to play, he knew which letter and number to push, and with three quarters, he could play it nine times. He pushed the buttons over and over until the light told him there was no more money to be spent.

The Captain and Tennille's "Muskrat Love" began to play.

He didn't particularly like the song, but he loved the squeaky voice of one of the muskrats at the very end.

"Aw hell," Dave called from the bar. "Did you just play that goddamn song again?"

Brad hung his head and began to shuffle back to his seat.

"Here," one of the men at a nearby table said and handed him another quarter.

"Don't give him... " Dave began. "Well, at least play something else too."

Brad smiled and returned to the jukebox. The song titles listed beside the glowing buttons were written in pen making them difficult to read, but he tried. Mrs. Appleton, his first grade teacher, had taught him to sound out the letters and put them into words. He concentrated and read the first one. He had no idea what it said, the curly letters bled into each other, but he recognized part of the name under it-George. He had learned to spell George just this week. They had sung a song about George Washington in school. The lyrics spelled the first name over and over. "G-E-O-R-G-E Washington, G-E-O-R-G-E Washington," and he loved singing it, even though the name spelling part was all he remembered. His father's first name was George, but everyone called him Dave. Learning the song had even inspired a question on the way to the bar.

"Other people have same names?" he had asked. "What?" his father responded, his shoulders slumped over the steering wheel, his arm hung lazily out of the open window. "Other people are named Brad, right?"

"Yeah, that's right."

"But no one has my whole name, right?" "What?"

"No one has my same first name and middle name and last name, right?"

"No, they might."

That answer had filled his mind. He was just learning math, so he couldn't fully understand the numbers that came to him as he tried to figure out how someone else could have the same three names he did. One other person? Two? A thousand? A million? It was a lot to think about.

So, George. That seemed like someone his father would like. He pushed the buttons, and then thought about pushing them two more times.

"George Jones. Good choice. Here let me help," Jen, the waitress who bartended on Saturday mornings, was standing over him, pointing to a selection. "This one is good." Brad pushed the buttons. "And this one." Brad pushed the buttons. "You'll like those. You wanna blow bubbles?"

Brad nodded happily as Jen handed him some Hubba Bubba. He unwrapped it as he struggled back onto his stool. The stool tipped a bit and his father's hand shot out to steady it before he grabbed his son's pants by the waistband and lifted him up, never stopping his conversation or putting down his beer. Brad sat upright and held out the pink cube. Jen made her way behind the bar and held out her own cube.

"One," Jen said and lifted the cube a bit higher. "Two... three." They both put the gum into their mouths and began to chew furiously. Brad's cheeks puffed out as the gum seemed to swell, but he kept chewing until it was soft enough, then he pushed his tongue into the lump and blew. A tight bubble formed and he blew harder. It popped and he started over. Jen began blowing, a pink circle formed in her mouth. Brad blew again and his own circle formed. They blew and blew until the pink orbs were twice as big as a baseball. Then, Brad's popped. The gum sticking to his deflated cheeks. Jen kept blowing.

"Keep blowing," a man said from one of the tables. Two other men laughed.

"Yeah, blow harder," another man snickered.

Dave was watching too. Brad smiled as the men cheered Jen's bubble. It grew to the size of a basketball. The men whooped and slapped their hands on the table. Jen kept blowing until finally the bubble burst. Pink goo covered her chin and one cheek all the way to her thick, black eyelashes. The men shouted and clapped. Jen peeled the gum from her face and carefully picked it out of her mascara before wrapping it in a napkin.

"That was good," Brad said.

"Sure was," Dave added and ducked his face under his arm to snicker at the men behind him. They all laughed.

"Men," Jen huffed and threw the bundled up gum into the trash can under the cash register.

"Muskrat Love" was just finishing and Brad strained to hear the squeaky voice at the end.

The Company Store

The old song goes,
"I owe my soul to the company store."
The company store was torn down
Just last year.
I watched them do it,
I swear I heard the cries,
I might have seen an orb
If I believed in such things.
They were kept there for decades,
These souls,
owed,
paid for.
Where are they now?
They might have danced among the trees,
Had the trees not fallen to mountain top removal.
They might have settled into the valley,
Had the valley not been filled with sludge.

The churches have a theory, If I believed such thing,
That god took the souls, But how?
"I can't go," the song says.
Without their souls,
The miners are trapped.
Without the company store,
The miners are lost.
Without the mountains,
How will they find their way home?

17

Elevators

"Push the button," he says
and I'm transported back to a time when
I used to beg to press the button.
Today, the fun is gone.
We step into the elevator.
"Push G," he says and
I want to scream,
"I know, Dad! I know what floor
because I've come with you a hundred times.
I know to push the button!"
But I quietly push 'G' and the doors close.
I help him untangle the cord from the I.V. in his arm.
We go down to 'G'
for another test
for another result
for another doctor
teaching me about life

and death
and losing a parent
and cancer
and I want to scream.
The doors open.
He wheels his own I.V. out.
"Push that big silver one."
I push the button,
the automatic doors open,
and we go inside to sit in another waiting room.

18

Waiting

The Veteran's Hospital doesn't smell like other hospitals. It's got a musk to it like sweat mixed with antiseptic. It also feels different. There's a sadness all around, a heaviness. Other hospitals seem to take great pains to lighten the heaviness, but not the V.A. or at least not the V.A. where my father goes for chemotherapy.

"You ready?" We're on the park bench where he's taken to sitting for a few minutes every visit because he's too weak to walk the whole way from the parking lot.

"Almost," he answers and presses hard on the cane between his knees. He's not strong enough to walk the next hundred feet.

He stops pressing on the cane and looks out across the hospital grounds. The humidity from the recent rain doesn't help, so I sit and wait, watching the dozens of broken men, and a few women, shuffle, stumble, or stroll past us.

One man, I've seen at Dad's appointments, is sitting in his

motorized scooter just a few feet away. The smoke from his cigarette wafts towards us and I sigh. He takes one more drag and flicks the butt off into the grass.

"I guess I better hide these," he says as he takes the pack and shoves it under the jacket in the basket fastened to the handle bars of his scooter. I can clearly see at least two other packs of cigarettes similarly concealed there. He smiles as he motors past as if to say, "Isn't that funny? A man going to chemotherapy and still hiding his smoking habit." I don't smile back. His daughter, walking behind him, shakes her head and laughs awkwardly.

A young man, maybe in his early twenties, hobbles by us on crutches. I can see the stark difference in color between his right and left leg. His right one obviously not original. He's wearing a t-shirt and shorts. Had he been standing on a street corner, I would have thought he was out jogging. The ball cap on his head bears the army logo. He doesn't smile as he passes. Instead, I see him gritting his teeth against the pain I can only assume is coming from his prosthetic. He has no one to help him cross the street, no one to lean on. Dad begins one of his coughing fits. He pulls the paper towel, ever present in his shirt pocket, and wipes the spittle from his mouth. I let the young man struggle past us and hope that one of the staff sees him soon.

Dad stops coughing and tries to hide the paper towel before I see the blood stain. I look away to allow him to believe he succeeded. He tries to inhale and I can hear the fluttering of something not quite attached in his chest. A young couple walk past holding hands. They look even younger than the man on the crutches. They both walk freely, they seem strong, but I know that I will see them back in the chemotherapy waiting room later today. I've seen them there before, just once, and I worry that the strength I see in this young man will not be there after today.

"You ready?" Dad says and rises to his feet. I get up and follow him, measuring my steps so that I keep pace with him. I'm struck by the family joke me and my mother share whenever we go shopping with Dad. "He just leaves me," my mother would say as I walked with her and we both would watch my father with his long, powerful strides increasing the distance between us so rapidly that we barely have time to get out of the car before he was in the store. Today, I have to pause after every other step to allow my father to catch up. I can tell that he's concentrating on taking individual steps and not shuffling. I don't know why he bothers, but I'm glad that he does.

Inside, that heady musk greets us like an unwelcome visitor. The heavy silence pools at our feet as we walk to the first waiting room. Dad takes a number off the wall. He's number three and I wonder if it bothers him that he couldn't be first today. He always tries to be first. Recently, his numbers have been getting higher.

"Number one," the woman who takes the blood calls out from the open door of the blood lab. A man steps to the door. I can't tell what brought him to the V.A. today. I hope it's just for a checkup.

"Do you have a hearing test today?" I ask as we wait for number one to get finished.

"Yeah, at 10:00," Dad answers.

"Number two," the woman calls and another man goes to the door. He looks even healthier than number one. I'm happy for them both.

"I hope they don't have that chicken salad again," Dad says.

"I'll go out and get you something. What do you want?" "A chicken breast and a biscuit." Sometimes it's a hot dog with sauerkraut. On those days, I can just go to the cafeteria. They don't serve fried chicken at the hospital.

"Number three," the woman calls and dad struggles to his feet. I wait for the drawing of the blood and don't rise until he's all the way next to me; we walk back to the chemotherapy waiting room. The young couple is sitting there. So is the man on the scooter with the hidden cigarettes. The wait here is not long. They need to get the saline started soon so that they can get the chemo started by the afternoon. The waiting room empties as the patients disappear. I sit and watch the cigarette man's daughter start her knitting and I watch the young woman begin to pace up and down the halls. I start to read a Kindle book on my phone.

After a trip to the cafeteria for a soda and a couple of trips to the bathroom, when my book has lost its interest, I lament that the hospital walls block signals so I can't download an-other, after I've checked on Dad at least three times, and after a parade of people come in and out of the room, it's nearly time for Dad's hearing test. I head back to the chemotherapy room. Dad is in the same chair he's always in--the furthest from the door. He's watching the television on the swiveling arm attached to his chair.

Dad is already up and holding onto his i.v. stand. He rolls it past me and into the hall. "Let's go," he says and I follow.

The auditory lab is one floor down so we take the elevator. We get to the small waiting room down a long hallway and I take a seat under the television. Dad checks in and sits next to me. We wait together.

"You taking chemo?" an ancient looking man asks loudly from a seat directly across from us.

"Yeah, I'm on my third treatment. Already had forty radiation treatments. Now, I'm doing chemo," Dad says in that scratchy voice that is all he can muster since the tumor is partly in his throat.

The man nods politely even though I can tell he couldn't hear a word Dad said. The room falls into silence.

"Owens," a woman calls as she pokes her head out from behind a door.

"Yep," Dad rasps and pushes against his cane until he stands. They disappear behind the door. I pull out my phone and open my book. I read the same sentence three times and close the program. There's even less of a signal down here in the basement, if it's possible to have less than nothing. I sit and listen to the television above my head. I can see the bathroom across the hall and I go even though I really don't have to. I read the posters and the bulletin board posts. Evidently, there's a seminar called, "Living Well with Cancer" next week. I find that a cruel joke. I memorize the inner working of the human ear as it is outlined on a poster. I also learn that hearing is intimately tied to emotion. Sounds with an emotional attachment, actually provoke real emotion. I find that bit of information irritating as I sit and try to ignore the news report above me.

I can hear Dad's voice, raspy and weak, approaching the door so I stand and wait. He comes out and we head back to the elevator.

"See you at lunch," I say as he goes back to the chair farthest from the door. I go back into the waiting room. The room is emptier than before. Someone has switched off the television and I make it a point to turn it back on immediately. I pick up a magazine. I've read it before. I pick up another.

Nothing of interest. I pick up another. Boring. I pick up another. Read it. I go to a different table. There's a Reader's Digest from the 80s there. I take it and read about a man who was lost in the arctic for nearly a month and I peruse some mildly amusing anecdotes from real people. I learn how to grill watermelon.

Who knew you could grill watermelon? I'm fascinated with the concept. Wouldn't it dry out? Isn't watermelon mostly water? Has someone really figured out how to grill water? And if they've been grilling water since the 80s, why am I just now hearing about it? It's nearly lunchtime by the time I stop thinking about grilled watermelon. I head back to the chemotherapy room.

"What do they have for lunch?" I ask.

"Hey, Sherri," Dad yells toward the little office across from him. "What's for lunch?"

"I think, chicken salad," Sherri answers.

"I'll go out and get you something," I say as he winces. I leave the room and walk quickly out and to the parking lot. The traffic has picked up so it takes me a little while to get into the flow and leave the hospital. I head across the street to the Bojangles. When I get back, there are no more parking spaces. I find a space next to the walking trail; I'll have a long walk to the hospital and a long walk to get the car while Dad waits on the park bench, but I don't mind. The humidity of the morning has lifted and the day is bright and sunny. There's a breeze blowing that brings the smell of pine and some flower that I can't identify by smell. I stroll through the park and onto the roadway leading to the hospital. I walk past Dad's bench and into the building. The air conditioning hits me like a cold slap. I would prefer to sit outside. I think that I might be able to go for a walk this afternoon. Dad has nothing scheduled that I know of, but I won't. I'll just sit in the waiting room.

I take the chicken breast and biscuit back to Dad and wait until I'm sure he doesn't need anything else before I go to the waiting room. The room is quiet again. Someone has turned off the television. I turn it back on. I take out my phone and realize I didn't download another book while I was out. I've got to remember to do that. I guess I could go for a walk and download a book. I should go for a walk. I can. Nothing will happen. No one will even know I was gone. I can. Instead, I head to the cafeteria for a soda.

The smell of the food in the warming trays makes my stomach tighten and I realize I haven't eaten today. I look over the food. Nothing looks good to me, but I order a veggie sub anyway. I grab a soda and get in line to pay. There are two women working. The same two who are there when Dad wants a hot dog. I pick the one I know to be more friendly and I wait even though the other line is moving faster.

I arrive back at the waiting room to the sounds of Spongebob emanating from the television; a family has taken up residence in my usual spot. I don't mind. I head to the other side of the room, as far away from the flashing colors and playful music as I can get. I eat my sub and drink my soda. I kick myself for not checking for service when I was in the cafeteria and I open my book and close it again. I go to the bathroom. I walk down to the information desk and back. I read an entertainment magazine and try to determine why one actress wore the exact same dress better than another. I figure it's the camera angles and the bias of the reporter because I see no difference. I open the music files on my phone and plug in my headphones. I play some songs and close my eyes.

The familiar tunes drift in and out of me with playful accuracy. I let the music take me to a better place and I linger there. I feel happier, lighter, freer, and I can't believe that damn poster in the basement was right about sound being tied to emotion. I try to make a mental note to bring my iPod to the next treatment. Maybe that will help pass the time. Or I could download another book before then. I start to feel frustrated and impatient; my music has stopped. I just don't have that many songs on my phone. I think about replaying them but I don't.

I get up and walk to every table in the large room. There are no magazines I want to read. I look at the clock next to the television. Just three more hours. Then, I play the game I always do when I watch the clock. I start counting the seconds and I look away while I continue counting. I count for a while then I look back to see how well I kept time. I try and do the math to tally up my score and I try to count again. A full minute this time. Then, I tally, which takes another minute. Then, I count again.

And again. And again. I start to think about stories I could be writing. It takes until the late afternoon for my mind to realize that I could have brought my laptop and written a novel by now. I add my laptop to the list of things to bring next time.

The daughter of cigarette hider is still sitting in the same chair as when I noticed her this morning. Has she moved? The scarf she's knitting looks almost complete. I don't recall how far along she was this morning. I wonder if I should take up knitting. She looks so calm.

"Let's go," Dad suddenly says next to me.

"You done?" I ask stupidly. He's already walking down the hall toward the door. I take my time but I catch up. He sits on the bench as I go get the car. It's late afternoon and the breeze is gone.

19

...With Dogs, Clyde, Cindy, Spunky, Blue, Tillie

The memories. I used to think I was cursed with such a good memory. I remembered everything, but, recently, I find that my memory isn't sufficient. I can't hold it all. Things slip into the haze of time. Important things. I had a dog before Lacy. I remember now, only vaguely. How could I have forgotten?

When I remembered, I sat and tried to force the thoughts to congeal. They wouldn't. I know I had a dog, but that's it. I can't remember a name. I can't remember what breed. I can't remember anything other than there was a dog before Lacy. For some reason, it felt so important that I remembered. I thought I could ask Mom, but I needed to remember myself. It was important. I swear it was important.

And then, other things came. Other dogs. I had forgotten Clyde. The old golden retriever mix that was named for my grandpa's brother. He had lost an eye. I never knew how, but he had a massive, black scar where his left eye should have been. He was a tough old dog. He used to go with me when I would walk down the holler. I did that a lot after Lacy died, after Sam was killed. I would walk down the holler. Not going anywhere.

Not really, but still I would walk. Clyde would come with me. He wasn't a pet. Not exactly. He was a practical dog. My family from the mountains always had practical dogs. I never really understood why, but they did. Some of the dogs were hunting dogs. Some were just for protection. Clyde was evidently for protection.

I remember him lumbering ahead of me. He was old by the time we moved to the mountain, or he had seemed old anyway, but he always walked with me down the holler. I don't remember what happened to him. He's there in my memories and then he's not. I know I was young, but I feel it's important that I remember.

Cindy was a beagle mix that died under grandma's porch. That's all I remember about her. I know she was grandma's dog, but she never came to our house, she never wanted to play, so I don't remember anything else. She was there, then she died. Dad had to crawl under the porch and get her out after she died. I remembered that. Then we drove her up to the graveyard and buried her in the woods next to the road. She lived her entire life just a hundred feet from me and I have no memory of her except her death. How can that be? Me. The guy with the cursed memory can't remember something. It wasn't possible.

Other dogs began to creep into my consciousness.

There was another beagle named Spunky that dad found at the mines. Beagles had this habit of following their noses and often got lost in the mountains, or they found something better. I was convinced that was Spunky-he found something better in my dad. He found a man who fed him the best food he possessed and loved him unconditionally. He found a man that was truly a good man, not one who pretended to be good when others were around. You can always tell what type a person someone is by how they treat dogs. It was the primary lesson my father taught me.

Spunky disappeared into the woods one day, after staying with dad for years, and never returned. Dad said it was what dogs typically did when they died. They went off alone and laid down under the trees.

My uncle had a blue tick hound creatively named Blue. He was a lumbering dog, more legs than anything, but with a blue and black spotted coat that was just beautiful. He was trained as a coon dog, which meant he loved to chase animals up trees. We often heard him out in the woods after he seemingly treed a raccoon or squirrel or anything really. He was a goofy dog, but sweet, just like every dog I have ever known.

The only time I remember being bitten by a dog was when I walked by my cousin's house and her German shepherd, named Tillie, having just given birth to a litter of puppies, evidently thought I was threatening and lunged at me. There was a little knick on my back where one of her fangs barely broke the skin. I didn't blame her. She was protecting her babies.

These dogs, and so many others, surrounded me my whole life. I remember them as I do family. Some better than others;

some more fondly, but they were part of my life. They still are, and that is because of my father and his love of dogs.

"They eat dogs," Dad had said about the Vietnamese people, but I can't believe that all of them did. After all, we are people too and we adopted dogs. We made them part of the family. We put them in our memories, in our hearts. I'm sure that other people did that too, even the Vietnamese that my father never seemed to completely forgive for his time in their country.

"He's Crash come back," Dad had said about Luke, and I can understand why he would want that. And truth be told, maybe Luke was Crash. People believe far stranger things than the concept of a dog coming back to protect a man he had protected before, and Luke was nothing if not my father's protection. That little white dog protected my father from snakes, and delivery men, and neighbors, and even ants. No one could have come into my father's presence during those final years without Luke's permission. Maybe he was Crash, finishing the job he had started decades before-keeping my father safe for as long as he could.

20

Drowning Daddy

I remember when I was little, I wanted to be like my father. I wanted it desperately. He was strong, proud, and respected. He demanded respect, and not just from me, his only son. He demanded respect from everyone he met. I admired that. I wanted that in my life. As a child, I associated his respect with his height. He was always larger than life to me.

I guess that's not unusual, a child thinking their parent was huge, but I carried this idea with me well into adulthood, and into middle-age. My father was diagnosed with stage four lung cancer just after the first of the year. It was odd. He was still that giant in my eyes. He was indestructible. Cancer? Not possible. Incurable cancer? Can't be.

A round of radiation treatments seemed to prove my estimation. He took the radiation with the same strength and stoicism I had always known from him. Cancer didn't stand a chance. My father would beat it with ease. Then came the chemotherapy.

The first treatment was long and tiring, but he came through it with flying colors, just like I knew he would. Then he began to lose weight. His body became this fragile, hunched thing that I barely recognized. Even his voice changed. The doctor explained it was because part of the tumor was in his throat, but that didn't help with the shock. He changed so quickly that I didn't have time to adjust.

In the Veteran's hospital for another chemo treatment, I strolled slowly beside him while he balanced himself on a cane. I was at least four or five inches taller than him. How was that possible? I had wanted to be as tall as my father all my life, but I stopped growing at 5'10". He's 6'3". Or he was before the cancer. Is it possible that cancer causes you to shrink? It's an odd thought, and I suppose people wrestle with the figurative nature of the disease all the time. This was not figurative. He was shorter than I was. The laws of physics didn't apply to cancer.

I began to despair. Maybe he wasn't going to be able to beat terminal cancer after all.

"Push up," my father said as he leaned heavily on the cane that had become part of him. We stood in front of the elevator that would take him, and me, to another appointment, another doctor teaching us about cancer and, by extension, life and death. I pushed the button and I thought back to when I was little and I begged to push the button. I wonder how many times I've pushed elevator buttons over the years without even blinking. The doors hiss open.

I wait until my father hobbles into the elevator. "Push two," he says before he's even halfway in. I want to scream that I know which button to push. I want to remind him how many times I've taken these elevator trips up and down the hospital floors, but I don't. I push two. The doors close and I feel that familiar lurch as the car starts to move.

Later, after treatment and Dad going back home and me going to my home, he called to tell me he was getting baptized. Well, my father called, but my mother told me the reason.

"You're not mad at me, are you?" my father asked on the phone.

"No," I replied, wondering why he would think that. It took a while, after hanging up, to realize why he asked what he did. I called back, "Are you giving up?"

"No, just getting ready," he said and I felt empty. "You're coming, right?"

Of course I would come. I drove the three hours to get to the service, I sat through the sermon, uncomfortable with the intent. I sat next to my aunt Sadie, who inserted herself between me and my parents, for some unknown reason. I assume she wanted to be closer to her brother, but I couldn't help thinking that she would enjoy this type of ceremony. She was very filled with the mountain religion. I had come only because my father asked, so I scooted over to let her sit next to him.

The service took forever to start. In the meantime, the congregation flocked by us. Everyone commenting on how proud they were of Dad. They shook hands with everyone. My aunts, my uncles, my cousins, my mother, and me. Many of them just accepted that I was another member of the family and it didn't matter who I was. Others wanted to know.

"You're Brad?" one man asked. "I guess you don't remember me. Last time I saw you, you were this high," he said with one hand sideways against his belt and the other holding mine.

"Sure, sure," I said, cognizant of the fact that I was both lying and making no sense at the same time.

"This is your son?" a woman asked. I didn't catch her name. It wasn't important. "Well, he's all grown up." That's what happens after 40 I wanted to say, but I just smiled and shook her hand.

"Brad? Huh?" the pastor said with both of my hands in his. "You sure did grow up to be a fine looking man." I smiled again, thinking it was best not to comment because I had no idea how to relate to these people. In any other venue, this man might have been hitting on me. Here? Who the hell knows.

Finally, the handshaking ended, my mom passed around the liquid hand sanitizer, and we settled in for the sermon. I don't remember any part of the sermon. It was said in that familiar yelling, chanting, angry tone of the mountain ministers. I always tend to tune that sound out. It just doesn't get through. What I do remember is Sadie nodding enthusiastically next to me, and my uncle Terry, the Baptist preacher, behind me, putting his two cents in.

"That's right," Terry would say after the minister made a salient point that I ignored. "We all need that," he would offer. "Well, he's not bad at all," was one comment and I thought how odd until I remembered that mountain Baptists typically don't go to other churches. That's seen as disingenuous at best and a damnable sin at worst.

My aunt, Fayger, was almost driven out of the church where she had been a member for nearly fifty years because she dared to go to a funeral of a family member at another church and she was seen singing at the service. The pinched faced old men had actually convened a meeting to vote on whether or not to allow her to stay. She's still a member, so I guess she won.

Sadie's head nodding became so passionate that the pew began to shake with the force of her agreement. I couldn't help but wonder where Sadie's husband, Danny, was, the other Baptist preacher in the family. This seemed like the very thing that he would have pounced on. Having told us all that God would get us eventually, I would have thought that seeing Dad baptized would have been the proof he needed of his self righteousness. Thanks to the preachers I grew up with, I always viewed God as a type of hunter stalking His prey. I was the prey. And whether I wanted it to happen or not, God would get me. Shoot me dead when I least expected it, or possibly worse, zap me with a bolt from the blue that would make me just like all the Baptists around me. Whichever it would be, I knew, from birth, I had better be ready. So, where was uncle Danny?

"Danny has vacation Bible school today too," Sadie said beside me, a little too loudly. Of course, the preacher in front of us was asking for volunteers to man their own vacation Bible school, so I guess she felt it was the appropriate time to tell everyone where Danny was. At least that solved the mystery and I could focus on ignoring the rest of the service.

"If anyone here wants to know Jesus better, come up to the

front," the minister said and everyone turned to Dad. After all, that was the reason we were all there, to see Dad find Jesus in the river out back. Dad just sat there.

"You're supposed to go up there," my mother offered and nudged my father's too thin arm. The chemo was causing him to lose too much weight, and he had been skinny before he began the treatments.

"That's not for me," Dad said and remained planted in the pew.

"Anyone?" the minister continued and looked at my father. I wanted to tell Dad that it was indeed for him, but it wasn't my place to keep the ceremony on task. I envisioned God with his rifle site centered on my father. "Well," the minister continued, "We're all here today for Brother Dave." He beckoned toward my father and the service was back on track.

Dad pulled himself out of the pew and shuffled to the front, his clothes hanging off of him like there was nothing underneath. My heart ached for the powerful man I had always tried to immolate.

"He's lost so much weight," Sadie whispered to me.

"He just won't eat," I answer.

"Well, he can't," she said and I became angry.

"No, he just won't. He's got medication that treats the nausea and vomiting. He takes a pill to increase his appetite. He just says it doesn't taste right and he won't eat." I realized I was angry at my father. He was acting like a child. He knew he had to eat, but he just refused. Then, an episode from my childhood flashed into my head.

I hated fried eggs. Still do. I will eat scrambled eggs,

omelets, French toast, anything with eggs really, but I despise fried eggs. My mother knew this when I was little. Dad only wanted fried eggs. So, she would fix Dad's fried eggs and then scramble me some after. One day, she forgot and after frying Dad's she fried me one. She realized it when she was putting it on the plate.

"Oh, I'll fix you another one," she offered.

"No," Dad said. "He needs to eat what you fix. He'll sit here until he eats it."

So, I sat with the fried egg in front of me. It was Saturday. I only wanted to watch cartoons, and I'm sure Dad had things he wanted to do, but we sat at the kitchen table. The egg growing cold and rubbery.

"You ain't gettin' up till you eat it," Dad said firmly, rising to his imposing 6'3" height.

I sat. The morning waned and I sat. Dad went out to mow the grass. I sat. Dad went to the store to get groceries. I sat. The afternoon came. Dad ate a sandwich and looked at me. I stared back, the egg a stone cold puck in front of me. I remember him sighing heavily.

"Did you even try it?" he asked.

I shook my head. I wanted to say that I have tried before. I remember trying. Fried eggs are disgusting. Instead, I just sat.

"Well, you ain't gettin' up till you at least try a bite," he said finishing off his sandwich. Even now, nearly 40 years later, I can taste the bitterness of that one, single bite.

"O.K. go on then," he said as I swallowed the congealed, rubbery mass.

"Well, it changes your taste, doesn't it? The chemo?" Sadie

said next to me in the pew. I suppose that's right, in fact, I knew that to be the case, but it didn't excuse the fact that he was acting like a child. He needed to eat. "Has he tried marijuana?"

The question hung in the air as the sing-songy chant of the church choir's song reverberated off the stained glass windows. "What?" I asked.

"I've heard that's supposed to help with appetite," Sadie said.

"It does," my aunt, Jesse, said behind us.

"Do you know where we can get some?" Sadie asked me.

I shook my head. Is my aunt, the Baptist preacher's wife, really asking if I can get marijuana for my father? "Hmmm? Do you know where we can get marijuana?" she asked the people in front of us. Soon, the whole church seemed to be whispering about marijuana and who might have some for Dad.

The choir stopped and we all headed out to the river. The sky, a roiling bundle of gray clouds when we entered the church, opened up as soon as we stepped on the bank of the river. The deluge was too powerful for an umbrella. The wind whipped and the water flew in every direction. The congregation huddled under a tree near the water's edge as Dad made his way to the chair the minister set up for him.

"Let us pray," the minister said, seemingly determined not to cut the ceremony short, even in the face of God's fury. I ignored the prayer, focusing instead on the rapidly rising water. It was rushing along the shores pulling large clumps of earth into it as it passed, muddy and angry. The preacher finished and took a tentative step into the river. I watched him stumble and wondered how they expected my father, already so fragile, to navigate those waters.

"Brad, come out of there," Mom said as she pointed over my shoulder. I had taken refuge from the rain under the tree, close to the trunk, and had neglected to notice the vines of poison ivy snaking up the wood. I turned and a particularly poisonous leaf was staring me in the face. I stepped back and the slight protection the tree's canopy offered ended. The rain pelted against my skin and I shivered as I watched my father take his first step into the river.

I wanted to scream for him to stop. I wanted to say that his immune system couldn't handle the mud and mire he was about to be lowered into. I wanted to point out that the rain was increasing the chances of sickness every second we stayed here. I couldn't speak. I just stood on the bank and watched two men, one on either side, lead Dad toward the preacher waiting near the center.

My father looked terrified. I saw him stumble. One of the men caught him. They clasped hands. The other man linked his arm under Dad's. They fought against the current, determined to deliver my father to the preacher. The dirty, brown water swirled around them all. It fought against them harder and harder with every step, but they continued. The preacher stepped forward and met them. They all turned toward the bank. The wind was swirling so hard that I couldn't hear a word as the minister raised his hand high into the air. Dad crossed his arms over his chest and the preacher, helped by the two men, pushed my father into the swirling waters.

They began talking over the spot where my father had disappeared. I still couldn't hear. I stepped forward.

The river licked against my mud caked dress shoes. The rain, streaming down my face, blurred my vision. I stared at the spot in the river. Then, they pulled and my father came out of the mud. I let out the breath I hadn't realized I had been holding.

The congregation began to cheer and Dad's face produced a skeletal grin that almost seemed like the man I knew. They all walked back to shore. My mother rushed forward with too many towels. She kept heaping them on Dad until I thought he would buckle under the weight. She kept dabbing him with handfuls of towels all the way back to the car. I thought about offering to help him up the slippery dirt road, but I couldn't seem to get my hands to reach out to him. Others slid in between us and took him by the arms. At the car, we jumped in, waving hasty goodbyes to everyone, and they understood we needed to get him home and dry. I started the engine to drive back to the house and the rain stopped.

"I think the preacher pushed me under too far," Dad said as we made our way back up the mountain. He was snorting, trying to get the muddy water out of his nose.

"Are you warm enough?" I asked, my fingers on the heat controls.

"I'm good," he said.

We got to the house and Dad changed out of his wet clothes and Mom wrapped him in blankets and quilts under the car port where the sun was now warming the summer air. I sat next to him and watched him shiver under the pile of cloth. His spindly fingers protruding from the cocoon to wipe the cold sweat from his forehead. I could see his knuckles, knobby without the flesh around them.

I went into the kitchen and opened every cabinet. I went to the refrigerator and examined every item in it. I sat at the dining room table and sighed. Someone had put a grocery bag in the empty chair across from me. I could see a bag of cheese curls peeking out of the paper. I opened them and headed back to the car port.

"Cheetos?" I asked, holding the bag in front of him. He thrust his shaky, too-thin hand into the bag and pulled out a large handful. I sat next to him and waited until he ate all of those. Then, I held out the bag again. He took another handful. I sat and waited.

21

My Grandmother's House

The scent of cinnamon
hangs softly
in the air
at my grandmother's house.
The leftovers of uncountable
years of baking waft gently
in the background
sneaking through the
coal warmed rooms.
Sleep comes easily there.
There exists a decided absence
of modern noise,
save for the tender hum
of the ancient Frigidaire,
but it is that ever present
scent
that hugs the senses-

ferociously sweet,
intensely loving-
with grandmotherly familiarity.

22

Things Do Change

They tore down Haysi High School
Making way for nothing really.
They just consolidated
the high schools in the county.
Ervington had been the first to close.
Clintwood resisted,
There really was no choice.
Progress required change.
There is one high school now.
I haven't bothered to learn its name
Something about a view.
I spent so many days at Haysi High School
Looking out of the window
Hoping the view would change.
My father remembered when the high school was built
Back in the 50s
I remember when they added

A set of stairs down to the Student parking lot.
Now, the view is different
It's of the ridge.
Ridge View High School
That's the name.

23

The Second Christmas

My father was born on Christmas Eve. We always celebrated his birthday at his parents' house, then we would celebrate Christmas. It was a tradition, but dad passed away in October and mom was not in the mood to go to his mother's house by Christmas. So, mom and I spent the first Christmas without dad watching movies at home. We didn't even decorate. There just didn't seem to be a need, or desire. Now, nearly a year later, I sat in mom's living room and wondered what we would do this year.

"You wanna go shopping tomorrow?" Mom asked suddenly from the doorway.

"Sure," I answered.

"I thought we could get a Christmas tree."

I nodded and watched the rest of the movie I had been watching. The next day we went shopping.

"We going to get a real one?" I asked on the way to the stores.

"Well, we could," Mom responded and I knew that meant she didn't want a real one. They were too much of a mess, and her mother had always been worried about the possibility of fire. Mom had inherited the same concern. One year, while mom was at work, I went out into the woods and found a small pine tree. I cut it down with the axe I used to split wood for grandma, and I dragged it back to the house. I stuffed the trunk into a bucket and filled it in with rocks and dirt before I placed it in the corner of the living room. When mom got home, her only comment was, "Isn't it a little too big?" I knew that meant I should get rid of it, and I did. We never had a real tree after that.

"What about that one?" she asked, pointing to a deep green one that was about eight feet tall. It was sitting on a platform in the middle of the garden section of Wal-Mart.

"It looks good," I answered and began looking for the correct box among the stack of boxes.

"We could get these too," Mom said, holding up a plastic container of ornaments. They were all black and white.

"Yeah," I answered. "That would be pretty." "Do you think we need color?"

"We could get some silver too."

"Yeah, that would work. With white lights."

We piled the tree and all the black, white, and silver ornaments we could find into the buggy. Then, we found a couple of strands of white lights and checked out.

"You want a milkshake?" Mom asked as we passed by a drive-in. "Sure."

We drank milkshakes and tuned the radio to a station playing Christmas music all the way home.

"Where do you want to set it up?" I asked as I unloaded the SUV.

"We can put it in the arctic entrance," Mom said, and I smiled. She had taken to watching reality shows about frontier living in Alaska. Evidently, all of the houses in the wilderness of the state had an arctic entrance in front of the house to keep the heat in when they had to go outside. Mom began calling her sun room the arctic entrance.

I set up the tree in the far corner of Mom's arctic entrance and began to string the new lights. Soon, I was hanging the ornaments. Black, white, and silver balls, White and silver bows, beaded silver garlands, and I discovered that mom had even bought a new star for the top of the tree.

"You want any help?" Mom asked from the kitchen where she was cooking dinner.

"If you want," I called back, nearly finished with the decorating. Mom came out and looked at the tree.

"I think we need more garland," she said as she began to hang ornaments.

When we finished, the tree was elegant, beautiful, and did not have a single ornament from our lives before on it. On the third Christmas, Mom brought out the old ornaments and her favorite tree skirt, but we kept the new star on top.

They Took the Mountain Away

We drive along the winding roads,
much like we've driven them my entire life.
The mountains rise up on both sides,
in places,
in others,
there is a mountain and a
sudden,
steep
drop off.

We crest the mountain,
much like we've done my entire life,
and it is gone.
The sky is too big.

"They took the mountain away," I exclaim.

"Coal," my mother says.

The coal needed to be extracted,
I guess.
There was a need for it,
I suppose.
There was nothing to be done,
so the mountain is gone.

"They took the mountain away," I muse out loud.
"Jobs," my mother says.

They needed work,
it's a simple as that.
They had dug as far down as they could,
that's a fact.
It's easier to take the top off,
digging is dangerous.

The sky is bigger without the trees,
without the mountain,
and the sun is too much in my eyes.

25 ▮

Three Breakfasts

"Y'know, when I was young, I used to eat two breakfasts, sometimes three," Dad's voice filled my memory. He had said this suddenly, breaking the silence of the warm summer afternoon long ago. I knew that he wanted to tell a story, so I waited. I shifted in my chair and settled in for the tale. He began:

"I used to get up well before sunrise. I wanted to eat with dad before he went to the mines. I'd sit and eat gravy and biscuits, bacon, eggs. Then, dad would head out. I would go up, most mornings, and see about Papaw. He'd be getting breakfast ready and I'd eat again. Gravy and biscuits, bacon, eggs. Then, when I knew he was okay, I'd go back home. Everyone else was getting up then, and I'd eat with them before we headed out to school. Gravy and biscuits, bacon, eggs."

Two breakfasts, sometimes three. It was a nice story. I liked it very much, and I thought about it often over the years. Of course, in my mind, through the shadow of memory, the words were truncated. Not as polished or forceful as they had been on that day long ago. But it was still a nice story, even with my own faulty memory reconstructing it. The specific words didn't seem to have much relation to me, like most of dad's stories, other than a nice story about my father's childhood. Dad loved to tell stories like that. I had a hundred of them in the stores of my mind. I couldn't recall them on command, most of the time. I would just be going about my business during a typical day and something would happen and I would think of one of dad's stories. They were always nice. Always comforting. Now, as I sit and watch my uncle, dad's brother, fix biscuits and gravy, bacon, eggs in the kitchen just a few rooms away from where my father had died just days before, I think of the three breakfasts.

The story is like a land mine now. I stepped on it the moment I saw my uncle. I remember, so clearly, on certain mornings, usually in summer, when dad would have the day planned for me well before sunrise. I always knew which days these were. He was loud in the kitchen. I always thought he made extra noise to wake me up on purpose. So, most of the time, I would get up. Sometimes I would lie in bed and hope that dad was just being clumsy. On those days, he would come in my room and tell me that breakfast was ready.

I would get up either way-on my own or with dad's help-and make my way to the kitchen where biscuits and gravy waited. I never wanted to eat such a heavy breakfast at such an ungodly hour, usually around 4:00 am, but it was what he always fixed. We would eat and he would let me know what I was in for.

"I'm heading to the mine," he would say after a sip of coffee. "You want to go?"

I would always nod as I ate because it wasn't really a question. He needed an outside man whenever he had to go into the mine, and I was the designated outside man, ever since I had a panic attack the first time I went underground. Then, when I was finished, he'd take the last sip of coffee. He always seemed to finish his coffee just when I finished eating. I never much thought about it back then, but he always did. It was as if he had the whole day perfectly timed. He'd set the cup in the sink and I'd take my plate over too.

Back then, mornings, well before dawn, in the mountains were always so quiet. What noise there was-crickets, frogs, early birds-seemed to melt into white noise. I never seem to remember them. When I visit mom now, and I go outside early enough, I can hear them, but I don't think of them otherwise, can't conjure the exact sound. It's an odd sort of hole in my memory.

We would get into dad's truck and the noise I do remember was the radio. Country music. The engine's soft hum. We would head off the mountain. Dad would light a cigarette and the smell of his truck is in my memory. Coal dust, stale smoke, greasy tools behind the seat. I could smell them all. I still can.

Sometimes, when I'm in a certain place, I can recognize the smell. The last time I remember smelling dad's smell was in a garage in the mountains. I was waiting for mom to get an oil change and the smell hit me when a man opened the door to the work area. It was there-the intermingling of smoke, sweat, grease, coal. I thought of dad's truck.

We would always stop at the bottom of the mountain, at a little convenience store.

"You want anything?" Dad would always ask and I would always say no. Then, he would come back with two biscuits-one for him and one for me-usually sausage. I'd take the biscuit and nibble on it all the way to grandma's house. I was usually finished when we started heading up grandma's mountain road.

The dirt road leading to grandma's was rough and the rocking of the truck was anything but gentle. The exposed rocks, the large furrows, the intermittent spray of gravel made for an interesting ride. By the time we got to grandma's I was wide awake-finally. Dad would pull up to the house and we would head inside where grandma was at the stove stirring gravy. We would walk in and sit at the kitchen table.

"You want an egg," grandma would ask.

Dad would usually say yes and I would say no. Dad would sip another cup of coffee as I spooned some gravy on a biscuit. We would sit and eat and have small talk. Grandma would tell us about dad's brothers and sisters and their families. Dad would usually laugh about something. His laugh is another thing that has become murky in my memory. I remember it. .. imperfectly. It's there, somewhere in the recesses of my mind. I have a sense of it. I know the feel of it, and it makes me smile. The exactness is gone though. It was like a giggle and a gaffe and a slight snort, but that's not completely it. When he was being mischievous, the laugh took on this deep, guttural, sinister chuckle that never failed to make me laugh with him.

No, not a chuckle, a sound that mimicked a chuckle. Like a comedic villain in an old western.

When we finished eating we would head home and I would go back to sleep for a while, usually another hour or two until the sun came up. Then, the day would start. I used to dread these mornings. I wanted to sleep in on the days that I could sleep in. I didn't want to get up so early and spend hours, before sunrise, driving off one mountain and up another. It always seemed like such a chore, but I always did it.

"You want an egg," my uncle asks as he notices me come out of my room. The land mine goes off and a thought occurs to me. It's as clear as any thought I have ever had in my life. It's so powerful that I can't swallow. The emotions stick in my throat like a poorly chewed meal. It's only then I realize that when I was young, I used to eat two breakfasts, sometimes three.

Brad Owens is an author and visual artist living and working in the Appalachian Mountains of Southwest Virginia and East Tennessee.

Born in Grundy, Virginia, and raised, mostly, in Haysi, Virginia, Owens has an insider's perspective of the Appalachian coalfields; however, his unique perspective comes from formative years in the suburbs of Chicago and his pursuit of higher education.

Owens completed a Master's of English and Master's of Fine Arts in Studio Arts. He uses his love of the written word and his passion for art as the catalyst for his work, combining his talents to produce singular works of art in book form.

9 798218 447588